The
DAN SULLIVAN
Question™

It is not about you. This is something everyone often forgets when helping a client. Unless you frame the conversations around the client, you will never demonstrate clarity, confidence, and capability. I have asked The Dan Sullivan Question hundreds of times, from priest to multi-billion-dollar investors, and I always get the same response: "What a great question!"

John Culbertson, Cardinal Partners
Charlotte, NC

The foundation of our entire business is the D.O.S. Our associates do not begin client meetings with anything but this approach. One client commented, "... I came in to the room assuming you were going to try to 'sell' me on your company. Two hours later, I had discussed the core issues and aspirations I had in my business future. I told you things I later couldn't believe I had discussed."

Bruce Thorne, Corporate Protection Group
Belleville, ON

Dan's question has simplified my approach to helping others achieve their goals, simplify their lives, and put them on a never-ending path of continual growth. It is the simplest and fastest way for them to gain clarity about their future. Dan has captured the essence of our being with this simple question.

Gary Klaben, Coyle Asset Management
Glenview, IL

Integrating Dan's question into my conversations with prospects and clients has radically changed the perception of my professional practice in the marketplace. Departing from the traditional approach of focusing on data, the question enables me to quickly create a relationship that is deep and meaningful, helping our clients to become instantly clear, confident, and capable. Asking this question has radically changed the way my firm operates.

Mindy Jones, Mindy N. Jones CPA, P.C. and Scottsdale Strategy Group
Scottsdale, AZ

Building meaningful relationships in today's highly commoditized world is increasingly challenging. True relationships are built through creating value, expanding trust, and helping develop bigger futures. Dan's D.O.S. Conversation is an essential component in creating any relationship. Dan's wisdom and insights are amazing!

Doug McPherson, McPherson Enterprises, LLC
Falls Church, VA

Asking this question communicates that you are interested in your client's future and not only their future relationship with you. My closing rate with this strategy is around 95 percent, but my anxiety level in the initial meeting has been reduced by about 150 percent.

Dan Taylor, Advisor Freedom
Charlotte, NC

When you can know in the first 15 minutes of a conversation how a person feels pain and aspiration – and, therefore, whether you can lead them out of one and toward another – that's the kind of nourishment that can cure anything.

Jennifer Summer Tolman, Second Summer Inc.
San Francisco, CA

The Dan Sullivan Question is a brilliant tool. It allows us to have an initial meeting with prospective clients and automati-

cally makes the meeting all about them. This question has become an integral part of our business for creating value for our clients. It's not unusual for prospective clients to ask us why their previous advisors haven't asked them these questions before. At that point, they realize that we are all about them and not us.

Ron Rogé, R.W. Rogé & Company Inc.
Bohemia, NY

D.O.S. has made a dramatic difference in our sales process and allowed us to differentiate our organization. We are able to build stronger relationships with our clients, as we have a better understanding of their needs, desires, and motivations. This question has directly resulted in the development of new products and intellectual capital, growing our revenue by an additional 40 percent last year.

David Engel, Innovative Graphics Group
Toronto, ON

Simply put, Dan's question transforms the way my clients think about their circumstances. It helps them quickly and easily transition from a preoccupation with their concerns to a positive mindset where they also recognize new opportunities. Most important, this tool can be used over and over again. Any time a concern or issue arises, this question is an effective tool for bringing about clarity and certainty. It's ideal for breaking through the paralysis that exists when opportunity is obscured by a myopic focus on the dangers one faces.

Elizabeth G. Norman, CFP, Retirement Specialists, Inc.
Brea, CA

Twenty years ago, my sales training taught me to open the relationship by talking about me and why I am a person of value and have an idea worth sharing. Using this method, I was reasonably successful, performing in the top ten percent of professionals in my field. When I learned this powerful question, my income quadrupled, and I am now in the top one percent in my field. Learning that it's not about me, but, rather, about them, revolutionized my business. The great part is everyone gets more of what they want.

Jeff Huston, Freedom Solutions
St. Cloud, MN

Since we have begun using the question consistently, we have seen a tremendous impact on our business. When working with new clients, it immediately separates who wants to do business in a transformational way from who is just looking for the cheapest price. Our relationships have strengthened to the point that we virtually eliminate the competition because no one else is like us. Our hit ratio on new business opportunities has increased from the 50 percent range to the 90 percent-plus range. Our client retention is almost 100 percent. This question may be the most powerful question ever asked.

Bill Kliewer, BKCW Insurance
Killeen, TX

If there is any secret behind my success in being named one of the top wealth advisors in the country, it is that I really get to know my clients well. It is The Dan Sullivan Question that has given me this great skill and advantage.

Joseph Janiczek, Janiczek and Company Ltd.
Greenwood Village, CO

Printed in Toronto, Canada. November 2017. The Strategic
Coach Inc., 33 Fraser Avenue, Suite 201, Toronto, Ontario,
M6K 3J9.

This publication is meant to strengthen your common sense, not
to substitute for it. It is also not a substitute for the advice of your
doctor, lawyer, accountant, or any of your advisors, personal or
professional.

Library and Archives Canada Cataloguing in Publication

Sullivan, Dan, 1944-
        The Dan Sullivan question : just asking will change your
life / Dan Sullivan.

ISBN 978-1-897239-17-9

        1. Self-actualization (Psychology) 2. Success. I. Title.

BF637.S8S835 2009   158.1   C2009-902553-1

Contents

A Note To Start.

Throughout this book, I refer to a "program" for entrepreneurs. It's called The Strategic Coach® Program, and you can read more about it on page 85. The Program develops and expands from the continual asking of the "special question" that is described on the following pages.

I had a college professor who said, *"Answers are a dime a dozen. What's rare in this world is a really great question. What's yours?"*

I came up with my mine in 1982 and loved it from the very first moment. Since then, I have built my life and my business around it. Along the way, I discovered that thousands of other individuals have found the "special question" equally motivating and useful in building theirs.

None of this would have occurred without the encouragement of my partner, Babs Smith, who always tells me that this is a really big deal.

The 23-Minute Answer.

One day in August 1998, I answered the phone, *"Hi, this is Dan Sullivan."*

The person on the other end said, *"Dan, thanks for taking my call. Could you tell me more about your program?"*

A member of my sales team had asked me to talk to a "hot prospect," a referral from a long-time client. The man was almost sold but just wanted to have a brief talk with me. He would make up his mind after I explained how our program would work for him specifically.

"I'm 90 percent there. I just want to hear it from you. I'd like you to explain it before I decide."

I replied that before explaining anything about the Program, I'd like to ask him a question:

"If we were having this discussion three years from today, and you were looking back over those three years, what has to have happened in your life, both personally and professionally, for you to feel happy with your progress?"

When I finished, there was a long silence. It was uncomfortably long, but I didn't say anything else.

Then he answered: *"Well, three years ago, I was a complete and total alcoholic. Nothing in my life was working. I had dug myself into a deep hole. So it's taken me three very hard and long years just to get back to ground zero. And over the next three years, I have to make some amazing progress — not only in my business, but in every area of my life."*

When he started to talk, I looked at my watch. He talked for 23 minutes straight, without my saying a single thing.

When he finished, he said, *"Well, Dan, your program*

sounds pretty good. You've answered all the questions I had on my mind. I'm ready to sign up."

Whenever I recount this story, especially his final comment, I always get a big laugh. At first hearing, it seems like a weird, almost nonsensical thing for him to say.

Most people shake their heads when I ask, *"Did I tell him anything about the Program?"*

"No," they say. *"He did all of the talking. It was all about him."*

But, then, invariably, someone will say something like this: *"No, you told him everything he wanted to know about your program. Namely, that it was going to be about him, not you. That's the biggest thing he wanted to know."*

People want clarity, confidence, and capability. I tell this story because it illustrates a truth about today's world and the marketplace: People want the conversation to be about *them*. They want to be asked about what *they* want.

What they want, I've discovered, are three things: clarity, confidence, and capability. Clarity about their future direction, confidence about what they've already achieved, and the capability to achieve bigger goals.

By asking a question — a special question — and listening for 23 minutes, I provided this man with all three of those benefits. Because I asked him the right kind of question and listened to what he had to say, he felt clearer, more confident, and more capable. And because he felt that way, he wanted to sign up for my program.

My contention in this book is that the question I asked is the most important question you can ask anyone. I believe it's the most important question in the world. Again, here's how it goes:

"If we were having this discussion three years from today, and you were looking back over those three years, what has to have happened in your life, both personally and professionally, for you to feel happy with your progress?"

In order to convince you to use this question for yourself, I'd like to analyze the conversation I just related. There are many important things to learn from it. By grasping what happened with this man on the phone, you can transform your approach to your whole future.

Let's break the conversation down into five parts. Each part contains a powerful psychological and practical lesson. Each lesson represents a lifetime capability that you can easily and quickly master.

Part 1: I provided an answer that was a question. The lesson here is that you shouldn't answer someone else's question unless you've first asked the special question that I asked in my story. Here's why:

The prospective client was expecting me to answer his question with a sales pitch because that's what everyone expects. And, invariably, the answer that people get is something that has been completely rehearsed.

In fact, the whole world today is about rehearsed

answers. Everyone is competing with everyone else to have the cleverest, most persuasive "answer." Billions of answers every moment, everywhere on the planet, are all competing for everyone's attention. The shouting keeps getting more insistent, and the volume keeps getting higher.

So in a world where everyone is competing with their answers, how do you differentiate yourself from everyone else?

With a question.

But not with just any old question.

The question I asked immediately and permanently differentiates you from everyone out there who is competing with an answer — which gives it a unique power.

"If we were having this discussion three years from today, and you were looking back over those three years, what has to have happened in your life, both personally and professionally, for you to feel happy with your progress?"

This is the basic way to ask the question. It always has a powerful impact because it makes the person asked think in a way they most likely haven't before.

Part 2: I asked the question and then shut up.
This is absolutely crucial. Ask the question, and then don't say anything else until the person answers.

It's an unusual question, but it's easy to understand. I've never had anyone say, *"I don't understand what you're asking."* I've asked it thousands of times over the years, and everyone grasps what it means.

The special question is very visual. It asks people to imagine a point in the future. Then it asks them to visualize what the next three years are all about for them. It asks them to see what's most important to them over this coming period.

All you have to do is ask the question, and their imagination will take over. Their natural ability to visualize will do all the work. If you say anything more before they answer, it interferes with their imagination. Just ask the question; they'll do the rest.

Many people respond, "Wow, that's a really great question." A successful trial lawyer told me, "That's the best question anyone has ever asked." Frequently, people will say, "This is really a deep question. Boy, that really gets me thinking."

Part 3: Jack answered the question.
In doing so, this future client, whose story I tell at the beginning of the book, probably gave me the best answer of his life. That's because it was the best question he had ever been asked.

Actually, I've discovered that there are three different ways people respond to the question. The best way to describe these three are as Users, Confusers, and Refusers:

Users: These are the 85 to 90 percent of people who answer the question pretty much the same way as Jack did in the story I recounted. They don't all talk for 23 minutes, but they do provide a substantial answer. Many people who have mastered this question report that the ensuing conversation can last an hour or more. And it's a great conversation, one of the best that you can have with anyone.

Confusers: These are individuals who do not have a future that they can imagine. Their minds either don't work in a visual way, or they are so confused about their past, present, and future that they can't create any answers. In some cases, the question helps them to break out of this. If not, asking the question at the beginning of a conversation helps you to recognize that there is nothing you can do for them.

Refusers: In my experience, up to five percent of the people will never answer a question like this. I call them Refusers because they do not really want to tell you anything about themselves or their future. This is fine because it saves you a lot of time that would be wasted attempting to create a relationship where none is possible.

It surprises many people that only one out of 20 individuals — at most — refuses to answer the

special question. But these same people, when
I ask *them* the question, always answer. In fact,
they are eager to do so.

The vast majority of people immediately see the
question as a unique and valuable opportunity to
think about things in a new, better, and different
way. It's rare that they get to think and talk in
this way.

The person who asks them the question is creating great value for them. For many people,
there's nothing that could help them more.

If you're the one to ask this question of a person who
understands its worth, you automatically become one
of the most valuable individuals in their life.

And even those who refuse to answer the question, or who are confused by it, will never forget
the question. It stays with them. I remember
one man in particular who was hostile when I
asked the question, saying, *"I don't even know
you. Why would I ever tell you anything about
my future?"*

My approach when this happens is to thank Refusers for their time and say, *"I appreciate the opportunity to ask this question. I wanted to see if there was any way I could be useful to you in your future. Since you don't want to tell me anything, there's nothing that I can do for you."*

With that, I end the conversation and leave. This is a shock to the other person because I am actually rejecting them, not the other way around. In many cases, they try to get me to come back, but I never do. They get one chance, and that's it. There are thousands of great people in the world who would want the opportunity to answer the question. I want to get on to them.

In the case of this particular man, I encountered him several years later at a business conference. He came up to me, all smiles, and shook my hand. He said, *"Do you remember when you asked me that question and I refused to answer? I couldn't get it out of my head for six months. The fact that you just got up and left really jolted me into realizing what a jerk I was. I just want to thank you. It really turned me around."*

One way or another, the question always does good things.

Part 4: The question answers many questions.
After Jack had talked for 23 minutes, he said that I had answered all of his questions about the Program. In actual fact, I had created the opportunity and framework for Jack to answer his own questions.

I believe that's what everyone is looking for.

The biggest challenge for everyone living today is how to adjust to a continual increase of complexity in every area of life. There are always more things to think about, and everything is speeding up.

There are many reasons for this complexity, technological change being the biggest. But, whatever the particular reasons, all of it causes three problems for most people. They are in danger of experiencing greater confusion, isolation, and powerlessness as the world around them continually changes.

For many people — even the most successful and advantaged — much of what happens that is new doesn't make any sense. Compared with how they remember previous times, today's world is much more confusing.

At the same time, they feel more isolated with this growing confusion. There is no one around them who can clarify things and make the changing world understandable.

The combination of growing confusion and isolation makes many people feel powerless to change their lives in a positive way. It's a vicious cycle. As things change and life speeds up, the compounded sense of confusion, isolation, and powerlessness deepens. This doesn't happen all at once, but rather by degrees. One way to measure the increase in the problem is by the number of questions individuals have about their future that they can't answer.

And no one else in the world can provide the answers for them.

For a growing number of people today, there are no "answers" from the outside that solve these three problems of confusion, isolation, and powerlessness. This is why there is a general "crisis of leadership" in most areas of life. Those who are in charge don't have answers — cannot have the answers — that people find useful for what lies ahead in their lives.

More and more, in a complex world, the answers that people find valuable will be their own. These will come from the inside, in response to the right kind of question.

"If we were having this discussion three years from today, and you were looking back over those three years, what has to have happened in your life, both personally and professionally, for you to feel happy with your progress?"

The question provides a framework that enables people to simplify their personal complexities.

Confusion is transformed into clarity when they answer what has to have happened for them to be happy with their progress.

Isolation becomes confidence when they realize that they can clarify their own future. The moment that people have a sense of personal direction, they immediately feel connected to the world around them.

Powerlessness transforms into capability as a result of their new clarity and confidence. In the case of Jack, he made an immediate decision and an investment.

All of these personal transformations begin to occur whenever individuals answer the question. There are no external answers in the world that have this effect.

But the special question always does.

Part 5: The question leads to decisions and achievements.
Jack had recovered from the worst effects of his alcoholism by not drinking. But he was now stuck, not knowing what to do next. Freedom from doing something bad does not automatically translate into greater freedom to do something good.

As soon as he answered the special question, he signed up for my program. Once in the Program, he made a long list of improvements he wanted to make. Over the next three years, he made amazing progress, and he's made even more since then. As usually happens, his actual progress was greater than he envisioned when he answered the question.

Whenever I saw him over those three years, he always said, *"I can't thank you enough for that discussion."* A discussion where I only asked a single question.

This has happened with thousands of other people who have answered the question. Many of them, in turn, have learned to ask it of others. This single question has led to millions of decisions and achievements in many places over the past ten years. In every case where people have answered the question, they immediately gained a sense of clarity, confidence, and capability that was missing before.

None of these answers came from me, or from other people who asked the question, because the special question creates the framework for individuals to create their own answers. It leads to a powerful discussion that can be created in no other way.

The framework for the discussion actually has two separate dimensions. The first relies on people's imagination. The second relies on their emotions. Everything I've related up to this point is the result of asking the first dimension of the special question.

In the next section, I'll explain the second dimension of this framework, but before doing this, I'd like to explain the crucial factors that make the "special question" work so well.

Four ingredients that have to be there.
Over the years, many people have heard me say the special question when I was giving speeches. They immediately went away and tried to use it based on their memory — but they often get it wrong. Then they tell me that the question doesn't work. However, it was their version of the question that didn't work. They had left out one or more important things.

The special question always works if you are careful to include four crucial ingredients. Each one has a powerful psychological and emotional impact. When all four ingredients are included in the question, the impact is transformational.

- *"If we were having this discussion":* If they agree to the idea that you are having a meeting and discussing things at some point in the future, it also means that they are okay with having a relationship with you. In other words, they are agreeing right up front that the two of you can be working together — *on something* — in the future.

- *"Three years from today":* This takes them out of the present to a specific point in the future. The moment their mind goes there, to a specific time period, they immediately gain a new perspective. Right now they are surrounded by complexity. But three years from now, in their imagination, they are free and clear of their present circumstances and issues (see question 8 on page 78).

- *"Looking back over the three years":* Now you are having them look at the present from a superior future vantage point. When people do this, their thinking immediately simplifies in a dramatic fashion. They quickly see what's important in the present and what's not.

- *"For you to feel happy":* The biggest thing that everyone is striving for is their own custom-designed happiness. Everything we want to gain, everything we want to leave behind, is for the sole purpose of increasing our happiness. And we want this to happen in every area of life. We have many measuring sticks in our brains. "Feeling happy" is by far the most important and permanent one (see question 9 on page 81).

As you go through the book, you will read about different examples where individuals are modifying the question for specific situations. In every case, these modifications only work if they include these four crucial ingredients. And when they are included, these modifications always produce great results.

Now let's jump to the next level.

The Great Conversation.

The second dimension of this discussion is called The D.O.S. Conversation®. Here, there is the possibility of a great ongoing discussion that can continually transform how people organize their lives for the better.

I've discovered that it's easier for people to create their most important answers if they can do their thinking inside a particular structure that makes use of their most powerful motivating emotions.

Dangers, opportunities, and strengths.
The acronym D.O.S.® stands for dangers, opportunities, and strengths. Here's what the whole question, both dimensions, looks like:

"If we were having this discussion three years from today, and you were looking back over those

three years, what has to have happened in your life, both personally and professionally, for you to feel happy with your progress?

Specifically, what dangers do you have now that need to be eliminated, what opportunities need to be captured, and what strengths need to be maximized?"

This second question taps into deep and powerful emotions. We all experience life emotionally before we make sense of what we're feeling. Even the most rational individuals start their thinking process on the level of their most powerful emotions.

Making use of fear, excitement, and confidence. Three emotions, in particular, motivate most of our thinking and achievement. Over the years, I've experimented with other possibilities but these three provide the most positive and motivating answers:

The first is *fear*, the fear of losing things that are important to us. These are the dangers.

The second is the *excitement* of gaining new things that are important to us. These we call opportunities.

The third emotion is *confidence*, from capabilities and resources we already possess. These are our strengths.

The raw material for everyone's daily thinking and activity consists of these three emotions — fear, excitement, and confidence — as they relate to our existing dangers, opportunities, and strengths. The D.O.S. Conversation uses these motivating sources to create motivating answers. It's how our emotions and minds naturally work together.

The D.O.S. Conversation builds a framework around this motivating process inside each of us so that our emotions and imaginations, in alignment, enable us to create increased clarity, confidence, and capability.

Every time the special question and D.O.S. are used in combination, they provide personal simplicity in a world of complexity.

What most occupies all of us every day.
When people think about their future in terms of D.O.S., everything becomes simpler. These three categories, tied to powerful emotions, cover most of what concerns the majority of people on a daily basis. They fear the possibility of losing important things. They are excited about the possibility of gaining new things. And they feel confidence from the things they have already achieved and possess.

They are already thinking in terms of three years into the future because of the special question. Now they can think about these three years just in terms of dangers, opportunities, and strengths.

When this simplicity takes hold, they become focused and truthful. All the mental clutter and noise disappear. There are just a small number of issues that they see as important.

I have experienced the focused truthfulness that emerges in The D.O.S. Conversation hundreds of times. Others who have mastered the conversation report the same thing. It always occurs when people focus on their most important dangers, opportunities, and strengths.

It seems that the opportunity is too important for them not to tell themselves the absolute truth about their situation as they see it. It is the special question and the D.O.S. framework that sets up this opportunity for them. They don't want to misuse or waste it.

All progress starts by telling the truth.
The moment people tell the truth about their D.O.S. issues, their progress starts. No matter where they are, they start moving forward with a sense of enthusiasm. The progress starts first in their minds: Their imaginations are engaged and their emotions are focused. Then it translates into their decisions to move forward, followed by actions and achievements.

Once D.O.S. is added to the special question, it creates a multi-dimensional discussion.

"Specifically, what dangers do you have now that need to be eliminated, what opportunities need

to be captured, and what strengths need to be maximized?"

People feel a sense of clarity, confidence, and capability regarding their future that had been missing.

Dramatically transforming how business is done. Over the past decade, I've taught thousands of people — both directly and through other coaches — to use D.O.S. in their businesses. It is a skill that can be grasped conceptually in the time it takes to read this book. It can be mastered in practice after a month of frequent use, after as few as ten experiences.

This new capability has dramatically transformed how these individuals create value for their own clients and customers. It works in every kind of business, with every kind of clientele.

Once they've mastered both the special question and The D.O.S. Conversation, their business relationships and organizations undergo a productive and creative change. Within a matter of six months, they're operating in a fashion that makes them immune to competition in their marketplace.

Here's the difference: As one of the entrepreneurs I coached to use The D.O.S. Conversation said, *"I've never had discussions like this in my previous 20 years. Before, I was just getting information. Now, I'm getting the real deal. Every time."*

Another entrepreneur told me this. *"They've never told anyone these things. They've never even told themselves that these were their central issues. It's amazing to see how surprised they are with their own answers."*

A third reported: *"Just having this conversation is worth tens of thousands of dollars to them in terms of their ideas and the actions they are able to take. And they want to pay me for my questions!"*

The three entrepreneurs I quoted were surprised by this response. But it happens so predictably that I consider it to be normal. I sense that people respond so powerfully to D.O.S. because the answers that emerge liberate their emotional power.

Emotional freedom in a complex world.
The three impacts of growing complexity in the world — confusion, isolation, and powerlessness — deprive many people of their emotional freedom. This deprivation occurs gradually, by small degrees, over many years. But when they enter the D.O.S. framework, the sense of emotional freedom comes back suddenly.

The combination of the special question and D.O.S. gives them a focused emotional power that many associate with being happy. Based on hundreds of D.O.S. Conversations that I have participated in, it certainly is what most people experience as excitement.

Before, they were feeling blocked, stuck, and frustrated for any number of reasons — all related to varying degrees of confusion, isolation, and powerlessness. Now, after The D.O.S. Conversation, they feel freed up in a way they had never before experienced. Before, the thought of the future was worrisome and a burden. Now, it is buoyant and motivating.

Just the special question on its own produces a uniquely valuable experience. In my discussion with Jack, I had not yet developed the D.O.S. question and framework, but he still remembers the simple question I asked him, and his answers to it, as a life-changing breakthrough.

Using D.O.S. to create a strategic plan and path. The addition of D.O.S. creates not only answers, but a strategic plan and path. For most people, it is the best plan they've ever had. It provides the best possible track for them to make both personal and professional progress.

I'd like to describe how I help someone create this strategic capability. My experience is that it can be done in a single hour, two at the most. It happens so quickly because the individuals already have all the answers they need.

I start by asking both questions, one right after the other:

"If we were having this discussion three years from today, and you were looking back over those

three years, what has to have happened in your life, both personally and professionally, for you to feel happy with your progress?

Specifically, what dangers do you have now that need to be eliminated, what opportunities need to be captured, and what strengths need to be maximized?"

This requires memorizing the questions, which most people can do in an hour or so. With a few weeks of use, the questions sound as natural as normal conversation.

For years after developing the D.O.S. framework, I would just ask the special question and let people talk for five to ten minutes. But asking the two questions together gets a much better and faster result.

Many people are not used to talking about the future in a focused way. They live in situations where daily conversations are almost entirely about the past and present. Few people they know can talk usefully about the future. This, of course, is one of their biggest frustrations.

D.O.S. gets to the central issues and truths.
When I add D.O.S. immediately after asking the special question, it focuses their thinking much better. They get to the truth of their situation — both what they want and don't want over the next three years — more quickly. Their answers are much more valuable and useful to them.

After asking the two questions — both special and D.O.S. — I focus first on their dangers.

What existing dangers do you need to eliminate in order for you to be happy with your progress over the next three years?

Some people don't like the word *dangers,* so I substitute *problems, worries,* or *concerns.* It's a personal preference, and I want to use the language that works for them. But for most people, dangers is fine.

One tip here: It's crucial to stress *the possibility of loss,* regardless of what word is used. The emotion underlying dangers that we want to utilize is fear: the fear of losing something that is very important to them.

When people are confused by complexity, fear is a great paralyzer. But when they get clear, fear becomes the greatest of motivators. The D.O.S. Conversation transforms fear into a great resource for achievement.

Always be recording and repeating back.
When the person starts to answer the danger question, I ask if I can record their answers for them. It's important to do this in order to capture their language, and so you don't miss any part of their answer.

When they finish answering to their satisfaction, I use my notes to repeat back to them what they said. My role here is not to offer any advice, suggestions, or solutions. My role is simply to let them hear all of their answers clearly and quickly.

Usually — especially with the danger issues — the result is that people feel more relaxed. They are relieved to have told themselves the truth. Until I asked the question and recorded their answers, their dangers were confusing to them, which always makes people feel tense and anxious.

Once I've repeated their answers back to them, I ask them to put their dangers in order of priority. Which is number one? Number two? Number three? I circle the written dangers and number them. Again, after doing this, I repeat back the order that they have given me.

Often, after this first stage of identifying and listing their top dangers, they will say something like, *"Geez, that feels good!"* And, of course, it does. When we go from confusion to clarity, it is a great feeling. When fear is transformed from a paralyzer to a motivator, it feels wonderful. In all of the D.O.S. Conversations I've participated in, my sense is that the other people are feeling a big boost of emotional freedom and power. And none of this has come from any answer that I provided. It has resulted from the answers they have created for themselves in response to my special question and the D.O.S. framework.

Gaining something new and important.
After the top three dangers have been noted and ranked, I go through the same process with the opportunities and the strengths.

What are the three biggest possibilities of **gaining something new and important** *that need to be captured? What are the three* **most important existing capabilities and resources** *that need to be maximized?*

It's important to be reading back what the individuals are listing as their key D.O.S. issues. This enables them to make a continual series of judgments and decisions related to what represents their best progress over the next three years — the progress that is going to make them the happiest with their improvement and achievement.

When completed, the D.O.S. framework consists of the top three dangers, top three opportunities, and top three strengths. These issues are best written on a sheet of paper that can be saved for reference. In many cases, I've had people hold onto this sheet for years because they consider it to be so valuable.

Transforming nine issues handles many others. I am often asked, *"What about the other D.O.S. issues, the ones that don't make it into any of the* *top three categories?"* My experience is that if the top three issues — nine in all — get transformed through decisions and actions, all the other issues also get transformed. And a great many things also get handled that weren't even identified.

What matters most here are not the issues themselves, but the increased clarity, confidence, and capability that come from identifying and transforming any one of them. What is occurring in this whole process is an imaginative and emotional transformation. As this occurs, all sorts of remarkably good things happen, many of them complete surprises.

The central objective of the special question and D.O.S. is to enable an individual to move from paralysis to motivation. The human brain and emotions are more creative and powerful than we know. The trick here is simply to get them moving in a direction that is crucially important to the individual.

Custom-designed route to the future.
By creating a framework of nine top D.O.S.

issues, people become committed to their own unique progress. Again, it is not my plan and path that are at work here. Rather, it is their own custom-designed route to the future, constructed from their own answers, their own personal truths, and their own central issues.

With these D.O.S. issues identified, we now have a framework for making decisions and a foundation for taking action. This is why there is a sudden increase in clarity, confidence, and capability. There is nothing more important in a person's life at this particular moment than the nine D.O.S. issues that are listed.

These issues represent the best personal truths that can guide an individual in improving all areas of their life right now. Most people recognize the importance of this moment of insight.

They often say something like, *"Well, there's nothing else I have to think about, is there?"*

Instead of being complicated, conflicted, and confused in their thinking, all of their intelligence, energy, skills, and creativity can now be channeled. Many people tell me that they've always been striving for this kind of focus. They've always been hoping for this kind of simplicity.

With the D.O.S. issues in hand, I now get the individuals to talk about each issue in greater detail. They are usually eager to do this because they are experts on each of these dangers, opportunities, and strengths. They are the only ones who know them first-hand. They know more about them than anyone else possibly could.

Here begins an extraordinary conversation, which, in many instances with my own clients, has continued for more than a decade. Once people acknowledge these nine D.O.S. issues — and take successful action on each of them — it always leads to new, "better" dangers, opportunities, and strengths further ahead on their route.

Best conversation about the future ever.
Most people tell me they have never had a conversation like this in their lives, and I believe them. It is the nature of our changing and confusing world

to inhibit both the opportunity and ability for most people to have good conversations about their future, let alone great ones like this.

Each of the D.O.S. issues is connected to many other issues and topics in people's lives. Once they identify these nine central issues, they continually become more insightful about many other connecting factors.

As the conversation proceeds, all of these other dimensions and considerations become integrated with the D.O.S. issues. I sense from my thousands of hours of participating in these conversations that there is a natural, organic growth process taking place inside people's minds as this conversation deepens and expands.

This overall integration of their most important thoughts, feelings, and aspirations is now focused on the future. They see their past and present as stepping stones. Because they have created a bigger future — in response to the special question and D.O.S. — much of what they have experienced and achieved becomes more valuable to them.

Getting their act together.

Of course, the integration occurs differently for different people. But everyone has a sense of a sudden breakthrough. Many people have described it as "finally getting my act together." The question now is what to do with the D.O.S. framework. There is usually a great eagerness to get started, to start making decisions and taking action.

This is also where the possibility of a unique economic relationship emerges — a relationship that can continually grow for decades. All of it is based on people's answers that come from the special question and the D.O.S. framework:

"If we were having this discussion three years from today, and you were looking back over those three years, what has to have happened in your life, both personally and professionally, for you to feel happy with your progress?

Specifically, what dangers do you have now that need to be eliminated, what opportunities need to be captured, and what strengths need to be maximized?"

The D.O.S.
Entrepreneurs.

As one of the entrepreneurs I've quoted has indicated, *people will pay for these questions, for these answers, for this framework.* To be able to design and construct, very quickly, a great and satisfying future is something people believe is worth investing in. An increasing number of people today are only too willing to pay for this capability and advantage in a world that is more and more frustrating for many others.

Worth a lot.
Back in the 1980s, using a rudimentary form of the special question and D.O.S., I was able to earn $200,000 a year. Life was much simpler then, and still I had an increasing supply of new clients for this focusing experience. In the much more complex and confusing world we live in today, the potential clients are multiplying daily.

What is it worth for people to have a process for moving from paralysis in their life to motivation? When you live in a society that is based on the ideals of continual improvement and progress, one of the most crucial experiences is to feel that you, yourself, are progressing.

What is it worth to move quickly from a sense of confusion, isolation, and powerlessness to one of clarity, confidence, and capability? Our world today offers many conveniences, pleasures, and benefits, but making this kind of personal transformation is more valuable than all of them.

What is it worth to achieve an ongoing simplicity in a world of escalating complexity? The pace of technological change is increasingly causing changes in every area of life. The ability to always be focused and simple in this world is an extraordinary advantage.

And, *what is it worth* to have an evolving personal framework for always being clear about your most important personal truths? In a confusing world with billions of external answers

competing for your attention, how valuable is
it to have a growing ability to be certain of your
own self-created answers?

The answer in each case is: It's worth a lot. It has
certainly been my experience that individuals
today are willing to invest a great deal in order to
gain all of these personal benefits.

The D.O.S. framework as a creative business.
So how does this economic relationship work? How
does it develop? I have been building this economic
possibility for more than 40 years and now have it
designed as a simple and satisfying process.

The economic relationship starts by transforming
the D.O.S. issues into short-term improvement
goals, and then into fast progress and achievements. I've discovered that most people don't
really have goals; they have wishes about their
future. For a wish or a hope to be a goal, it has to
be achievable and measurable, and it has to have
a deadline.

For example, where does the individual want to

be with each of the nine D.O.S. issues at the end of the next 90 days? The answer to this question takes D.O.S. from being a framework to being a practical plan and path. This is how ideas become achievements.

Progress not experienced without measurement. This is where measurement enters the process, for without measurement there can be no satisfying progress. For progress to be measurable, one of two things must be true: Either something is achieved that can be counted with numbers, or something is achieved that is a clearly defined milestone — it either happened or it didn't.

As soon as these measurable goals are established, we have a 90-day structure for an economic relationship. If everything inside of this structure moves forward, and there is measurable achievement at the end of it, this is something worth paying for. In fact, it's the best investment opportunity that people will ever have available to them.

It is invariably the first time in their lives that those experiencing the special question and D.O.S.

feel that everything crucial to their future happiness is being custom-designed. For their entire lives, they have always had to fit their futures into other people's systems and structures. This is the first time they get to think and act in a system that is uniquely their own. One of my D.O.S. clients many years ago told me, *"This is like a school. Only it's the best school that I've ever been in, because I am both the teacher and the student."*

Over many years, this same theme of a uniquely designed education has been expressed in dozens of different ways. My sense is that, in a world of greater and greater complexity — and the increasing confusion, isolation, and powerlessness that come with it — this is the only kind of personalized ongoing school that keeps getting better for each individual. It keeps getting more useful and more valuable.

It occurred to me after helping to create D.O.S. frameworks for hundreds of entrepreneurial clients that an entirely new industry was possible. The use of the special question and D.O.S. created a new economic dimension. This industry was made possible by the increasing desire of more people to have greater control over their personal futures. Year by year, they want to have more parts of their lives, both personal and professional, under their own design and direction.

This new industry was easy for me to explore and expand because all of my clientele were already successful entrepreneurs. When I came up with the special question and D.O.S., I already had direct access to more than a thousand of these enterprising individuals operating in 60 existing industries.

Entrepreneurs always motivated by freedom.
Entrepreneurs are the ones who create every new industry because they are always looking for new ways to be more in control of their businesses and their lives. Their biggest motivation is always increased freedom: greater freedom from restrictions, on the one hand, and greater freedom to create new forms of value that they can profitably sell, on the other.

Entrepreneurs, more than the vast majority of other people, dislike being constrained inside of other people's systems and structures. As a result, they are always looking for ways to bypass existing ways of doing things that have diminishing returns. They are always on the outlook for new approaches that expand their opportunities and capabilities.

The special question and D.O.S., I discovered, were a new capability that created new opportunities. The entrepreneurs I work with were — and are — always looking for new ways to help their own clientele. The D.O.S. framework was a simple, quickly-mastered process that made them and their companies more valuable as soon as it was used.

D.O.S. enabled these entrepreneurs to imagine and design their own better futures based on their own answers, their own personal truths. Their whole lives were about doing this anyway. The addition of D.O.S. enabled them to do this systematically and predictably. It provided a custom-designed growth process that kept getting better the more they took advantage of it. As long as they kept working inside of D.O.S., their clarity about their future grew stronger. Their confidence always increased. Their best capabilities got more valuable.

Everything in business and life improves.
The tangible results showed big increases in their income and profits. All areas of their personal lives improved, especially the relationships that meant the most to them. Quite quickly, they were able to spend their work time doing what they loved and did best. And, with their personal and business lives under greater control, they greatly increased their philanthropy, volunteerism, and community leadership.

Entrepreneurs' ongoing financial success within the D.O.S. framework enables them to purchase protections from the complexities that other people can't avoid. Their increased money enables them to acquire greater capabilities, both in terms of people and technology.

These D.O.S.-based entrepreneurs not only enjoy more freedom than people in general do, but are continually more free than other entrepreneurs who lack this framework and process. It is a competitive advantage that continually grows. The progress and growth are reinforced by constantly revisiting the special question and the D.O.S. issues at regular intervals. Those clients working with me, and with the other coaches in our company, return every 90 days to renew their focus.

Hundreds of D.O.S. businesses.
It was only a couple of years after I introduced the D.O.S. framework to my entrepreneurial clients that I got a big surprise, a marvelous and exciting surprise. I discovered that the D.O.S. approach was a highly contagious idea and capability. In a very short time period, hundreds of D.O.S.-based businesses emerged. The entrepreneurs who were my clients were using the framework with thousands of their own clients. They found this way of thinking so valuable for themselves that they were eager to use it with others.

These new businesses were created in dozens of different industries. This experience told me three things: that the approach was easy to learn, that my clients loved the benefits it provided to them, and that these were benefits they wanted to pass on widely and quickly.

Although these D.O.S. entrepreneurs were from different specialties, they found the approach equally useful. Each of them developed their own presentation style, but they all stuck to the logic and wording of the special question and D.O.S.

Financial advisors were early adopters.
Many of the first entrepreneurs to create D.O.S. relationships with their clientele were personal financial advisors. This makes total sense. Financial advisors are in a business that is entirely based on personal relationships that in many cases can last for decades. Their main business is getting people to take greater control of their futures, primarily through the use of products of one kind or another. But instead of attempting to sell products to their existing clients and new prospects, these advisors now began selling the D.O.S. framework first — with the products now becoming implementation tools. One of them told me that this single change of strategy transformed his entire view of his role and business. He said, *"I immediately went from being a peddler of products that anyone could sell to being a designer of other people's progress."*

By using D.O.S., hundreds of financial advisors have dramatically differentiated themselves from their competitors. The financial services industry throughout the world has steadily become more commoditized. It is increasingly difficult for advisors to differentiate themselves on the basis of commoditized products. But it is easily and quickly possible for them to do this permanently with D.O.S.

The primary strategy for these advisors now became to help their clients gain greater clarity, confidence, and capability *first* — with the sale of products becoming almost a *by-product* of this process. By doing this, they immediately changed the nature of their client relationships. The D.O.S. framework removes all the feelings of "being sold," or, worse, being manipulated, that historically have given financial advisors a bad reputation.

Dramatic differentiation from competitors. As a result of these changed relationships, the advisors' clients told them the truth about their futures. A financial advisor using D.O.S. gains insights into their clientele's aspirations that no product-based advisor would ever know about.

One financial advisor, after operating within the D.O.S. framework for a year, talked about the change it made: *"The difference with D.O.S. is so drastic; it's like my whole previous dealings with clients had been a guessing game of hit and miss."*

Within their transformed D.O.S. relationships, these advisors quickly created solutions that were more useful. They saw opportunities that were invisible to product-based competitors. They recommended strategies that took their clients by surprise because they were so insightful.

And this same quantum leap of capability happened with D.O.S.-based entrepreneurs in other industries. Regardless of the industry, there was invariably a sense of having made a great professional breakthrough.

In every case where D.O.S. was used, the clientele became more motivated to do business — and to do so for longer periods. The D.O.S. entrepreneurs were naturally more excited about what was happening to them, their work, and their future. And all of these transformations stemmed from the outcomes of the special question and the D.O.S. framework.

"If we were having this discussion three years from today, and you were looking back over those three years, what has to have happened in your life, both personally and professionally, for you to feel happy with your progress?

Specifically, what dangers do you have now that need to be eliminated, what opportunities need to be captured, and what strengths need to be maximized?"

Best way in the world of doing business.
Looking back over the thousands of successes that I know about, I can confidently say that the D.O.S. approach is the best way of doing any kind of honest business in the world. In every industry, it transforms the nature of marketplace relationships and solutions — and always for the better.

A few examples from different industries.
David Engel, a printer from Toronto, had competed in conventional ways in his local market.

By applying D.O.S. to his customer relationships, he became a master of direct response marketing, innovating proprietary strategies, methodologies, and products that he licenses to international advertising agencies, corporations, and suppliers. David says of this transformation, *"It always starts with D.O.S. Over the last ten years, I have created my own industry, with dozens of top customers looking to my company as their creative marketing supplier. I sell far more printing than I ever did before, but that is not what I go in selling."*

Philip Tirone was a million-dollar-a-year mortgage broker from Los Angeles. Before he took the D.O.S. approach to his business, he was working 80-hour weeks with no days off. He now markets his strategies for lifetime credit-worthiness to millions of consumers and to other mortgage professionals — while growing his own mortgage business. More important, he now has a full and satisfying personal life that would never have seemed possible to him before. Philip told me, *"When think about how I worked before, it's like a bad dream. I was a slave to a business that was never going to get more interesting.*

The only reward was money, and I probably would have burned out before I could've made much more. Now my life is based on creativity that will earn me ten times more, easily. And I now have a life. All because of the D.O.S. framework."

Joe Polish started off as a carpet cleaner in Tempe, Arizona, working, as he put it, "insane hours for stupid returns." Using the D.O.S. approach, he quickly realized that his best skills were in marketing — not only for his business, but for helping thousands of other cleaners across the country. As with Philip Tirone, Joe's strategies and methods are transforming an entire industry. His own personal success has been so great that the most successful cleaners now use his marketing process to grow their businesses. Enthused by this progress, Joe has now branched out to provide marketing innovations for clients in dozens of different industries.

Joe reflects on his D.O.S. journey: *"It just turns your mind around so that you look at everything from the client's perspective. You stop thinking in terms of your product, and start thinking in terms of their problems and solutions. I'm pretty bright and creative, but it wasn't until I took this approach that everything clicked."*

D.O.S. as a doorway to a new business model.
In each of these examples, it was the special question and D.O.S. that enabled these entrepreneurs to create their new business models. Each entrepreneur uses the D.O.S. framework to solve problems and capture opportunities for their clientele that would never occur to product-based competitors, and then sell their creative breakthroughs to many of these same competitors! David, Philip, and Joe — and hundreds of other D.O.S.-based entrepreneurs — continually go far beyond the boundaries of conventional thinking and methods. Just using the D.O.S. framework makes these individuals unique.

Each D.O.S. entrepreneur develops unique problem-solving processes within their D.O.S. frameworks. This enables them to focus entirely on the issues of their clientele without being constrained by "the way everybody does it" in their particular industries. They were all creative to begin with, but D.O.S. enables them to be practical innovators with expanding futures.

Breaking into new territory beyond the industry.
Every industry in the world, over time, becomes
organized around the attitudes and results of
average performers. As this occurs, commoditiza-
tion sets in because everybody is selling the same
things in the same ways, for ever-lower prices.
The D.O.S. entrepreneurs, in every case that I've
seen, quickly break into new creative territory
where the profits are higher because none of the
competitors can follow.

Creative solutions that no one else can provide.
Instead of trying to sell products as their main
objective and activity, *D.O.S. entrepreneurs sell
superior thinking, decision-making, planning,
strategies, implementation, and continual review
and improvement — all related to the client's
existing and emerging D.O.S. issues.* They sell all
of these creative "brain" skills within Unique
Processes™ that are custom-designed for each client
and customer. And as we have seen in the examples, they sell not only to their clientele but to
their competitors, who become ongoing buyers

themselves. Because these D.O.S. entrepreneurs are increasingly seen as the leading innovators in their industries, they sell far more products than was ever possible before they used the framework.

The special question and D.O.S. are a crucial doorway that enables entrepreneurs of every kind to enter a new world where they can be continually more innovative and valuable.

We live in economic times where people are increasingly judged by the new value they create in a changing world. In every case where individuals use the D.O.S. approach, they are seen by clients and customers, and by colleagues and associates who work with them, as the best value creators they know.

Throughout the business world, the emphasis is increasingly on "value creation." The hundreds of entrepreneurs I work with all know how new value is created. It all starts by asking the special question and then creating endless new solutions for their clients and customers within the D.O.S. framework.

Joe Polish, who says he started off as a "harried and hassled" carpet cleaner, describes the advantage he now has: *"D.O.S. for me is like a doctor having MRIs and CAT scans as compared with my competitors, who can only check their 'patients'' wrists for a pulse. I can always see dozens of new ways to solve problems and create opportunities for my clients, where they can only see what they've always seen and only do what they've always done."*

Questions About The Question.

The special question and D.O.S. are very provocative ideas for everyone who engages with them. Not everyone likes this approach, and some people can't or won't answer the questions. But no one can ignore the personal challenge that the D.O.S. framework poses.

Even when they understand the concept of D.O.S., many people still have dozens of questions about how, where, and why to use it. Here are ten questions that often arise and need to be answered before people feel comfortable using the D.O.S. approach.

1. Is this question only for entrepreneurs?
The answer is no. Any motivated individual can use the special question and D.O.S. with great results. I provide many entrepreneurial examples because for the past 40 years I have personally

worked with thousands of entrepreneurs in 60 different industries. The vast majority of them discover that there are extraordinary advantages to using this approach in their specific relationships with clients and customers.

For those who are not entrepreneurs, the D.O.S. approach brings equally gratifying results. The first step before using it with others, of course, is to apply both the special question and the D.O.S. framework to your own personal and professional future.

D.O.S. is a great new skill for every person, young or old, who is committed to being more capable. What I mean by this is that your own growth is a top priority — that you are working to change your circumstances in order to go to a higher level of achievement and impact.

If this describes you, then you will get a continual payoff from the D.O.S. framework that keeps getting bigger and better. Even though you may not be an entrepreneur when you start, you will think and act more entrepreneurially the more you use the approach.

2. What if I'm too scared to ask it?

I have entrepreneurial clients who knew about the special question and D.O.S. for ten years before they tried them for the first time. They say they could kick themselves for waiting so long.

Using the D.O.S. approach is generally awkward or uncomfortable for the first week or so. By the time you've gone through the experience ten times, it will seem natural to you — so natural, in fact, that talking to people about their future in any other way will seem like a wasted opportunity.

Once you're through this initial period of discomfort, operating within the D.O.S. framework is an increasing pleasure. You realize that D.O.S. automatically makes you useful to other people in ways that no other approach can match.

Everyone I know who uses D.O.S. tells me that it gives them a great sense of capability in all their relationships. There are two reasons for this. One, they are strengthening their ownership of their own future. Two, by using the question, they are increasingly surrounding themselves with people who are taking ownership of theirs.

The bottom line: One or two weeks of discomfort is all that separates you from possessing one of life's greatest capabilities. It will be a great advantage to you immediately, and it will be one that continually grows for the rest of your life.

3. What if the first ten people I ask refuse to answer?

My first short answer is that having the D.O.S. approach rejected ten times in a row has never happened. Thousands of individuals have been using the D.O.S. approach now for more than a decade. Few of them have experienced more than one person in 20 not being willing or able to answer the special question.

The second short answer to this question is that, right now, you might be surrounded to an unusual degree by people who are either distrustful or without future goals, or both. This can occur in situations where there is no creative or entrepreneurial activity. For example, inside a large bureaucracy, or in a location that is in economic decline. Most people in these situations are trapped in the past and in dead routines, and can't think very far ahead. Your asking them the special question will suddenly and painfully remind them of just how trapped they are, and they may resent you for doing this.

If this is the case, then it is crucially important for you to form as many new positive relationships as possible with future-focused people. The best way to do this, of course, is through the increased use of the special question and D.O.S.

My third, longer, answer is that you might be asking the special question incorrectly by focusing the person's answers so they relate back to you. Here's an example:

"If we were having this discussion three years from today, and you were looking back over those three years, what has to have happened in your life, both personally and professionally, for you to feel happy with our relationship and what I am doing for you?"

Notice how the question has become self-serving. Instead of putting the focus on the person answering, it puts it on the person questioning. If I were asked the question in this fashion, I would tell the person asking it to get lost. This is an entirely manipulative approach, and most people, consciously or unconsciously, will pick up on the fact that it isn't really about them. There are variations on this manipulative approach, and they all lead to an unpleasant and unsuccessful result.

The whole D.O.S. approach is based on the strategy that it's always and entirely about them, not about you. Much of the power of D.O.S. comes directly from the suspension of self-interest on the part of the person asking the question. In a self-centered world, this experience is both unique and liberating for those being asked the special question and D.O.S.

The more you practice the D.O.S. approach in this spirit, the more differentiated you will be in the minds of everyone you ask. You will seem uniquely different and extraordinarily useful. The first ten people you ask will be excited by the experience and grateful to you for it.

4. What if asking the question destroys the relationship and/or opportunity?

I am often asked this question by individuals whose daily work takes place in highly competitive situations — usually within organizations where increased status and power are the main motivations.

My answer here is that the D.O.S. approach never destroys anything useful, but it always reveals very quickly whether a situation or relationship is worth investing in. Some situations are win-lose arrangements where other people can only see themselves moving forward if you are seen to lose ground.

For example, if other people are manipulative and controlling, they will never answer the special question or respond to the D.O.S. framework. Never. In fact, if you even ask them the question, they will immediately see you as a threat and someone to be avoided. People who have secret agendas immediately recognize the D.O.S. approach as dangerous to their schemes because it would shed light on what they are hiding.

Relationships with these kinds of people are not worth any investment of your time, talent, or energy. The D.O.S. approach will immediately identify who these individuals are, allowing you to extract yourself from any contact with them.

On the other hand, D.O.S. also immediately reveals those relationships and situations that are truly worth your investment. By making D.O.S. a consistent and constant strategy, your life will quickly fill up with opportunities that move everyone's life forward in the best possible ways.

Summing up, then: The only thing that the D.O.S. approach will ever "destroy" are situations that are bad for you. And it will do it quickly.

5. *Why do I want to know about their issues that I can't solve?*
I often get this question from individuals who think that asking questions means that you have to take responsibility for the answers that the other people give them in response.

Again, it's important to realize that the D.O.S.

approach isn't about you — it's about them. It's not about what you are going to be required to do as a result of what they say. Just by asking the questions you are doing something uniquely valuable. You are not required to do anything else.

The whole point of the special question and D.O.S. is to enable them to see what their crucial goals and issues are. In my opening story, Jack didn't need me to solve his problems. What he appreciated so much about the 23 minutes that I let him talk was that he was able to be so clear about what was important to him over the next three years. I gave him a chance to think clearly in a way he had not been able to do before. Because of this, he immediately felt more confident. And because he was clear and confident, he also felt more capable. Thousands of people using the D.O.S. approach report exactly the same results from asking the questions.

If you are willing to try this, you will get the same positive results in your relationships, both personal and professional. Millions of people are looking for someone who can provide them with the opportunity to become more clear, confident, and capable. You can easily be that person.

D.O.S. enables people to go from being paralyzed to being motivated. When you think about the difference between being happy and unhappy, this breakthrough into motivation seems to be a central factor in what it means to be happy — in all situations.

6. Is this approach only good for personal, one-on-one relationships and situations?

The special question and D.O.S. can be used in any setting where people are interested in building a bigger and better future for themselves.

First of all, D.O.S. is great for any kind of one-on-one relationship. Think about it. What could be a more interesting and productive topic of discussion than what people want to achieve over the next three years? Having this topic as a main focus improves every personal and professional conversation in the world. Everything else that's worth talking about — past, present, or future — will emerge as a result of taking this approach.

But I have discovered, secondly, that the D.O.S. approach also produces superb results in group and team situations, both big and small. We not only have individual futures, we have collective ones as well. There is no better way of establishing a group future that everyone is committed to than through the D.O.S. approach.

An interesting insight: Dozens of the D.O.S. entrepreneurs I work with have discovered that a group's refusal, reluctance, or inability to answer the special question immediately reveals that the group members are not unified in their agendas and commitments. It's crucially important to know this so you don't entangle yourself in a group situation that is going around in circles or breaking apart.

One entrepreneur reported back on one such situation: *"In one week, I was making a presentation both to a board of directors of one company and to a committee in another. In both cases, they refused to answer the question — and the refusals were almost angry. In both cases, I quickly ended the meetings, telling them that there was nothing I could do for their organizations. In both cases, they tried to get me back, but I refused. And I am so happy and relieved that I did."*

On the other hand, if the groups and teams are cooperative and forthcoming, you can be sure that the use of the D.O.S. framework will lead to progress and success that everyone involved will be happy with.

8. Why three years?

I happen to love three years as a period for imagining and measuring future progress. Most people I've worked with also like this time period. It's the year after the year after next, and most people can visualize their progress clearly. I've also discovered that trying to imagine too far beyond three years is not effective. Things become too abstract and fuzzy. But in practice, the special question and D.O.S. are being applied to many different time periods — sometimes as short as a week. I've never done this, but others have with good success. The shorter the time period, of course, the more limited the goals and measurements need to be. But whatever time period is used, D.O.S. always works.

The issue here is: *What time period is most useful for the other person?* What time period is most likely to produce the most valuable and useful answers for them? Usually the individuals themselves will tell you the future time period that works best for them.

Example: Ken Arlen, a musician, orchestra leader, and owner of an entertainment company in Chicago has custom-designed the question for prospective customers planning special events that are very important to them. Here is how he uses D.O.S.:

"If we were having this discussion 90 days after your event, what do people have to say about this experience for you to feel happy with how you organized and put it on?"

Notice that nowhere in the question is there anything about him or his company. It's entirely about their event and how the people who are invited to it respond to the experience. Nor is there any reference to music. The customers are not purchasing music, but rather a great experience that others will enjoy and praise.

He then goes on to ask about the D.O.S. issues. What are they concerned or worried about? What big opportunities will come out of having a successful event? What resources and capabilities do they already have that will ensure this success? When I interviewed him on his approach, he said that it is often a half-hour into the discussion before the topic of music comes up. *"By that time, they are so excited about the event and so appreciative of how I have enabled them to think about it, that I don't even have to sell my services. In their minds, I've become their partner in putting the whole thing on. The whole topic about music and my price gets handled in a few minutes. And we always do a great job because we know exactly what our customers are striving for. My competitors in Chicago have no idea how I keep getting these jobs. And even if they did, they would never use the D.O.S. approach because they think the whole world revolves around them and their music."*

Ken's example has another crucial lesson: People are always buying "experiences" in their future that will make them happy. My own take is that we probably never buy anything else. Even when we buy a product, it's not actually the product that we think will make us happy, but the experiences related to our future use of the product.

9. Why the words "happy with your progress"?

Well, for one thing, most people like the sound of those words. That's because "happy with your progress" relates to everyone's number one concern in life. At all times, all of us are thinking about the future experiences and results that will make us happy. I'm not sure that we ever think about anything else.

Second, in everyone's case, there is only one expert who knows what will make them happy. No one except the individuals, themselves, know how to judge what will make them happy. That is equally true for me and everyone else. So if you want to know what will make anyone happy, you can only ask that person — and no one else.

Third, there can be a big difference in a person's mind between "progress" and "progress that makes them happy." We all make progress continually that seems normal and to be expected.

There's nothing special about it. Not making this progress would make us unhappy, but making it is something that we take for granted.

What we're after in our use of the special question and D.O.S. is the future progress in the other person's imagination that will be their biggest motivators — in other words, those achievements and results that will make them the happiest. And this person is the only "expert" in the world who can tell themselves and us what these are. D.O.S. ensures that you only talk to experts.

10. If I use the question consistently for 20 years, what will happen to me?

I'll answer for myself. By consistently asking and answering the special question and operating inside the D.O.S. framework since 1989, I have achieved a 40-times-greater income, and every area of my personal and professional life has been transformed in ways that I could not have imagined when I started.

And I personally know hundreds of entrepreneurs who have used the D.O.S. approach as a daily practice in their work and lives for more than a decade. They all report that quite amazing things have occurred, and most of them were surprises — all of them good.

If you follow their example, the single biggest benefit from using D.O.S. is that you will continually be more excited about the world and your life within it. If you consistently do it for 20 years, your practical success is likely to be similar to mine and theirs.

The cause for this increased excitement will be your ever-increasing usefulness in the eyes of other people who are growing because of the questions you ask them. Your sense of purpose and meaning will grow with each new person you help.

Depending on your role and goals, the D.O.S. approach will transform dozens, hundreds, or thousands of relationships and situations.

Wherever you are, you will be seen as a creative and positive force in others' lives. Many people will see their relationship with you as a top reason for their ongoing growth and success.

The positive impact you have on others will have a transformative impact on you, too. Seeing the continual progress that you help others to achieve will continually motivate your own. And you will live within relationships and situations on all sides that are moving forward in ways that are exciting, productive, and satisfying.

Others, seeing how you are using the special question and D.O.S., will follow your example, using it in their personal and professional worlds. This means that your positive influence and impact will extend far beyond just those you know directly. You will continually have a growing sense that you are making the world a better place in thousands of ways that you don't know about. In all of this growth and progress, you won't have to supply any of the answers. You simply need to ask the question:

"If we were having this discussion three years from today, and you were looking back over those three years, what has to have happened in your life, both personally and professionally, for you to feel happy with your progress?"

The Strategic Coach® Program.

My own use of the special question and D.O.S. with entrepreneurs has evolved since 1989 into a lifetime growth program for successful business owners. Over 18,000 individuals have participated in The Strategic Coach Program, some for over 20 years. In most cases, their time in the Program represents their greatest period of success and satisfaction.

The moment that entrepreneurs begin to operate within the D.O.S. framework, they develop new ambitions. These ambitions are above and beyond the goals and achievements that have already made them successful.

The first ambition is to be in an accountable growth structure and process where they can continually measure their personal and professional progress. They want to do this in the company of other entrepreneurs who are also striving for higher levels of capability and results. Strategic Coach® satisfies this ambition.

Their second ambition is to be in an ongoing community of D.O.S. innovators where they can continually learn new approaches and methods. By nature, these entrepreneurs operate "outside of the box" compared to the general population. Strategic Coach is a setting where they are among kindred spirits — highly successful kindred spirits with big goals. As one participant put it, *"Coach is the only place where I can be unabashedly ambitious and everybody thinks it's a great thing."*

The third ambition that these entrepreneurs have is to develop their D.O.S.-based businesses into much larger and more significant enterprises. And this continually happens, with increasing numbers of them creating new business models that transform existing industries and lay the foundation for new ones.

The Strategic Coach Program is well known in entrepreneurial circles as the *school* where "the best get better." The constant improvements that entrepreneurs experience are not just in business but in all areas of their lives. One of the most talked-about benefits is how much richer and enjoyable their family lives become.

At present, Strategic Coach operates hundreds of quarterly workshops in the U.S., Canada, and the U.K. New workshops are established on a continual basis. The vast majority of participants join because of the progress they have seen in other entrepreneurs already in the Program.

For many entrepreneurs, Strategic Coach is their permanent life process that encourages and supports growth and achievement in all areas of their lives. One individual put it this way: *"Until Strategic Coach, running my own business was always a lonely experience that was getting lonelier and harder the more successful I became. Now I have a place, filled with the best friends in the world, where I rejuvenate and refocus every 90 days. It's what was always missing. Now that I've got it, I'm staying for life."*

Participants derive many unique benefits from

Strategic Coach, but most report four big improvements: constantly increasing income and profits; significant and, in many cases, unbelievable jumps in the quantity and quality of free time; the ability to focus increasingly on their most productive activities; and an ever-increasing impact on the world outside of their businesses.

To qualify for Strategic Coach, entrepreneurs must have three years' experience as business owners and personal incomes in excess of $100,000 or £100,000. They must also be committed to their own personal and professional growth so that being surrounded by others with the same commitment will be an opportunity and pleasure.

I am the creator and designer of the hundreds of tools and methods that have evolved out of the D.O.S. framework. The team around me numbers more than 100 associate coaches and team members who are dedicated to each entrepreneur's growth and success.

If you qualify, register for the Program by calling 416.531.7399 or 1.800.387.3206. From the U.K., call 0800 051 6413. Or visit us at *strategiccoach.com*.